'Absolutely gorgeous . . . a beautiful, quirky, comforting little book.'
Annalisa Barbieri, columnist, *The Guardian* and *The Observer*

'I've found *Psalms for the City* charming, intriguing and challenging in equal measure. I'm tickled by the wit and wordplay. I love the illustrations.'
Edward Canfor-Dumas, author of *The Buddha, Geoff and Me*

'This book is a delight. Keeping quirky and cheerful, it suggests serious things without taking itself seriously. It could make even the most complacent sceptic laugh and think again.'
Richard Harries (Lord Harries of Pentregarth)

'This intimate, approachable book provides a collection of day-by-day songs, or psalms, that fit our busy contemporary lives. Always thoughtful, often celebratory, sometimes painful: these rueful verses – and their gorgeous, witty illustrations – build up into something both serious and delightful.'
Fiona Sampson, author of *Common Prayer* and *Come Down*

John-Paul Flintoff is a writer, artist and performer. His books include *How to Change the World* for The School of Life, and most recently *A Modest Book about How to Make an Adequate Speech*. *Psalms for the City* is his first poetry collection.

Psalms for the City

John-Paul Flintoff

Original poetry
inspired by the places
we call home

First published in Great Britain in 2022

Society for Promoting Christian Knowledge
36 Causton Street
London SW1P 4ST
www.spck.org.uk

British Library Cataloguing-in-Publication Data
A catalogue record for this book is available from the British Library

ISBN 978–0–281–08604–7
eBook ISBN 978–0–281–08605–4

10 9 8 7 6 5 4 3 2 1

Typeset by Fakenham Prepress Solutions, Fakenham, Norfolk NR21 8NL
First printed in China by HK Forwards

eBook by Fakenham Prepress Solutions, Fakenham, Norfolk NR21 8NL

Produced on paper from sustainable sources

Contents

Introduction

Some time ago, I started dropping into churches. Not just occasionally, but often. Near home, and further afield.

I was coming out of a breakdown. In therapy, I'd found myself talking a lot about faith. Specifically, about *lacking* faith – in myself, in my future, in everything.

This was odd, because I hadn't thought of myself as a person who had 'faith' in the first place.

After my therapy sessions, I'd drop into a nearby church to think about what I'd said and heard. Why? It was cheaper to go into a church than a café.

I had no idea what to do, and felt sure that I was doing it wrong. But I watched somebody kneel silently in front of a particularly beautiful Mary and Jesus, and when she left I did the same.

I found the experience powerful, in a way I can't begin to explain.

Another day, overwhelmed with anxiety, I dropped into a church that provided leaflets containing suggested prayers for a variety of occasions.

I learned some of the prayers by heart, and when I felt troubled I repeated them, to silence my self-critical thoughts. I carried that leaflet for months, until it fell apart.

I mentioned these developments to my therapist, and to others I knew to be religious. As well as Christians (I didn't know many), these people included Jews and Muslims.

It would be dishonest to say that everybody was encouraging. But most were.

One in particular comes to mind: a Muslim friend encouraged me to get baptized, and after I did she asked me to read prayers to her in hospital, as she was dying of cancer. She asked me to read at her funeral.

I chose Psalm 137. It had become a favourite, as had psalms generally.

Many of the people closest to me are Jewish. I could imagine that my becoming a practising Christian might be uncomfortable for them. I looked to the psalms as an inheritance we can share.

One Jewish friend read me a modern translation of his favourite psalm. I can't easily explain why this was so much more moving than if he had read me a favourite poem. It just was.

Though brought up in no particular faith, I'd become familiar with the Bible when I studied English literature. I'd also studied illustrated psalters.

My favourite, the *Luttrell Psalter*, is a priceless book commissioned by a prosperous family, combining the psalms of David with illustrations of biblical scenes and of everyday life in medieval England.

Much of what we know about how people lived 500 years ago comes from marginal illustrations in the *Luttrell Psalter*.

It occurred to me to create a modern psalter – to illustrate the psalms of David with images from my own part of London in the twenty-first century.

I would draw people in churches, I decided – but also in synagogues, mosques and temples. I'd draw scenes from the Bible and from everyday life.

But as well as being an artist, I'm a writer. I decided I'd write my own psalms.

To be clear, I realize they are nothing like the real thing. But they mean something to me, and I hope they might mean something to you.

Before I had my breakdown, I bought any number of books by Buddhists. *The Little Book of Calm*, *How to Be Zen* – that kind of thing. At the time, I would never have bought a similar book by a Christian.

Christianity seemed either bonkers (too many unbelievable things to believe) or merely repellent (like Homer Simpson's goody-goody neighbour).

I hope that might change – that people of no religious background will feel comfortable buying similar books by Christians – a *Little Book of Grace*, or *How to Be Forgiven*, that kind of thing.

This book of psalms is my attempt to help make that happen. It's designed for anybody. It's for Christians who fancy a 'pilgrimage' around London. It's for Muslims, like my friend, who are open to witnessing and encouraging another person's faith tradition. It's for Jews who love the psalms, and might want to write their own. It's for Buddhists, calm or not.

It's for *humans*.

My uncertain engagement with prayer and churches has given me consolation, joy and strength. I hope you will enjoy my attempt to share that.

Psalms for the City

Chocolate Box

When she was little,
a girl I know
carried a box upstairs
into my office.

It had previously contained
chocolates from the supermarket
at Finchley Road.

But now, she confided,
it contained
God.

She asked me to look after it.

I did, I have.

Now, God, I invite you to squeeze
into this book,
for others to discover you.

Psalm Psunday

The Lord showed strength of his arm
when he invented the psalm.

(The P is psilent.)

Being psalmless
is relatively harmless.

But to find where your pulse is
try reading someone else's.

Rise above the hubbub
of the city and the psuburb.

Want to feel calm?
Read the twenty-third psalm.

King David wrote an armful.
Make your brain psalmful!

Sing a New Song

Sing a new song.

Sing at the piano, with the key that's not responsive,
spread your fingers beyond an octave.

Play harmonies with your highs and lows.
Paint rainbows.

Plunk, goes the broken key.
Plunk.

Sing a new song,
sing a new song.

Annunciation at Grenfell

Driving on the Westway, just past Ladbroke Grove,
I saw them silhouetted by the sun.
When I was young, the middle one arose
Before me every day as I left home,
Soared above Kensington New Pools (long gone).
Held up the sky above Westbourne Park Road.
I never noticed it. Reminds me now
Of Mary facing Gabriel, painted
In a church I went inside once. Between them,
In the distance, Christ hauled his cross.

Mary, Five Minutes Later

But what was Mary doing
Five minutes before?

What was she doing
Five minutes later?

These too were
Prefigured.

Part of your plan.
But what were they?

And what about me
Right here, right now?

A Pea, in Kew

Planet Earth
is a pea
on the platform at Kew

The moon
is a crumb
on a staircase in Richmond

Saturn
is a cup and saucer
in a cafe in Hackney

The sun
is a pumpkin
on The Wrekin

And the nearest star
is a car
in Pennsylvania

Don't Belong

My father took Grandpa to Midnight Mass,
And I came too. I'd never been before.
I was excited, mystified. And tired.
They rose and walked to the altar rail, and
I came too. I took the bread and drank wine.
But when the service ended, Grandpa said
I should not have done it, wasn't allowed.
Gentle Grandpa, never angry, angry.
I sat in the back of the car, resolved
To reject what had made him like this, hate
The church, its rules, people, hocus-pocus,
Hymns, pews, God, steeples, organ music, choirs,
Crosses – especially crosses. All that.
But said nothing. Not for decades. Sorry.

FAQs

Q. How can anyone
come to believe
the worst
of a great ally
and then
set it aside?
> A. Only if you believe
> the worst
> can you
> set it aside.

Q. Does physical distance
remedy anything?
> A. Going far
> from the source
> of your pain
> can't remove
> the pain
> in your heart.

Q. How to believe
two completely
opposed ideas?
> A. Paradox
> is contained
> only in the mind.
> There's no other way.

Smiting Time

Isn't it time you started smiting?
My life has been full of resentment.
But when I think of writing it down
I feel ashamed of myself, and convinced
That if anybody deserves smiting, it's me.
But I've been here before.
Have mercy on me.

Room 320

If you get the bus towards
       Marylebone Station, it's just a short walk
              to the psychiatric hospital.

If you ring the bell,
       and they let you in, say you've come
              to see the man in room 320.

If you go up to the third floor,
       you'll probably find
              his door is open. They're keeping watch.

If he looks (as he will)
       depressed and anxious,
              tell him this before you leave:

You are loved.

Grateful

Practise gratitude, they said.
You'll feel wonderful.

I tried, and it was pleasant enough
to list good things.

But something was missing.
'Thank you' seemed empty

Without a target.
Like a love letter to nobody.

I had much to be thankful for.
But who was I thankful to?

Lifetime

I'm born, I cry
I blink, I eat
I sit, I laugh
I hold my feet
I stand, I walk
I'm at the fork
I choose my path
I soon regret
I jump through hoops
I learn, I run
I fly, I boast
I fail, like most
When others die
I hide my cry
I see you not
I ask for what
I haven't got
I'm on my knees
I don't know how
I see you now.

Verbal

In the beginning was the Word
and the Word was with God.
And they walked together in Kensington Gardens,
in the pleasant evening, smelling jasmine.

But the Word was lonely,
so God took some letters from the Word
and created the Sentence.
And the Word was delighted, rejoicing.

'You are of one flesh,' said the Lord.
And their sons and daughters were many,
like dots per inch, merging into something greater.

Their sons and daughters were the Noun,
and the Adjective, and the Verb.

And the generations of the Verb were this:
The Verb begat the Action.
The Action begat the Consequence.
The Consequence begat the Narrative.
The Narrative begat the Question.
The Question begat the Answer.
The Answer begat the Dispute.
The Dispute begat the Falsehood.
The Falsehood begat Irony.

And God walked with Irony, and used Irony for his mysterious ways.

But Irony could not speak to God,
because the Lord God
knows everything.

Pray for You

W. said, 'Do you mind
if I pray for you?'

I thought he meant
on Sunday, at his church.

'Yes, please.'
I was grateful for the offer.

And right there in Knightsbridge
he placed his hands on me.

One on each shoulder,
on the straps of my rucksack.

'Jesus,' he began . . .
And I don't remember the rest.

Once, I'd have been
mortified, or cracked a joke.

Not this time.

Next Year

Shema Israel
they've shut the shuls

Bismillah
they've barred the mosques

Hail Mary
there's no worship in churches

Next year
Next year
in Jerusalem!

Seasons of Google

I can't help noticing the changing seasons
As I walk around on Google Street View. It's spring,
Over here, but elsewhere trees have leaves on.
I can't help noticing.

Not Exactly Babylon

i.

Seventeen-forty-five.
Was that Bonnie Prince Charlie's big year?
When Harrison dreamed
Of measuring longitude with clocks.

Ticktock, ticktock, ticktock.
They built the church
Pandemic has shut down.

Days would come, days would go.
The church's north side slide, fall wonky.
In they prayed, out they went.
Harrison's bones were laid to rest.

On a bench outside, now,
I can't get my head round it, frankly.
Sky falls dark, moon rises,
Over the church where I was baptized.

Souls by the thousand,
Unseen, tip their hats and cross themselves.

ii.

At the height of lockdown
        I walked to church
And took a photograph through the
        Stained glass
Of the dark interior.

Only the font was clearly visible,
        Though shadowed by the bright
Windows opposite.

I studied the photo carefully,
        Thought of my baptism
Less than a year before
        Over that same font,
Water trickling off my head.

And I thought of the exiles
        By the rivers of Babylon
How they sat down and wept,
        But might have stopped
Weeping, if somebody
        In Jerusalem, equipped with a camera,
Had taken a photograph
        Of the dark interior
Of the Temple.

And sent it to them by email
        As I sent this to my friends.

Consequences

Christine said
when she was training
trainees were invited to write
the first line of a psalm
addressed to God

Then fold the top of the paper over
and pass it along
for someone else
to write the next line

Like a game of Consequences
the Bible itself is the work
of many hands
written on scrolls

It can be shocking
when a line of ecstasy
is followed by vengeance
or gnashing of teeth

But unlike Consequences
despite the confusion
you can read the Bible and the psalms
in hope and confidence
that the writers were sincere

Why would you address God
any other way?

Breathing Haiku

God, meditate me.
Tune your breath, like a Buddhist

In.

     Then.

       Out.

         Then.

           In.

Twelve

The patriarchs said:
Did you admit you were powerless?

The matriarchs said:
Did you come to believe?

The prophets said:
Did you make a decision?

The seraphim and cherubim said:
Were you searching and fearless?

The cloud of witnesses said:
Did you admit the nature of your wrongs?

The desert fathers said:
Did you become willing?

The holy martyrs and saints said:
Did you humbly ask?

The apostles said:
Did you make a list?

The archbishops said:
Did you make amends?

The Orthodox and the Catholics said:
Did you continue to take an inventory?

The Protestants and agnostics said:
Did you seek, through prayer and meditation?

My friends said:
Did you have a spiritual awakening?

I said, yes.

Rejoice in the Lord

Rejoice
>you magnolia trees of Hampstead.

Rejoice
>you cherries that blossom on the estates of Longberrys, off
>>Cricklewood Lane.

Rejoice
>you dandelions on the allotments.

Rejoice
>you window boxes.

Rejoice
>you ivy in the shadows.

Rejoice
>you lawns of the rich.

Rejoice
>you houseplants that get too much water.

Rejoice
>you parched weeds of the dual carriageway to Brent Cross.

Send down your roots
>into the clay and compost of London
>and rejoice.

Books Have Wings

I read page after page of a book
　　　　about writers and artists
　　　　　　　whose creativity, the author said,
　　　　　　　was closely related to periods of mania
　　　　and frequently took the form
of religious enthusiasm.

I found this quite depressing
　　　　and hurled the book away,
　　　　　　　across the room, through the window
　　　　　　　and through the beautiful blue sky, to the
　　　　uttermost parts of the sea.
Its pages the wings of angels.

Thirty-two Boroughs

Thirty-two boroughs call to you

Darken Barking & Dagenham
Barnet, darn it
perplex Bexley

Torment Brent
(more strongly) Bromley
abandon Camden

Not avoiding Croydon
cause squealing in Ealing
enflood Enfield

Thirty-two boroughs call

Itch Greenwich
scratch Hackney

In Hammersmith & Fulham
they clamour, they're sullen
sneering, in Haringey

Harrow's sorrow
Havering's quivering
Hillingdon's pillaged and
Hounslow is crouched low

Thirty-two boroughs

It is written
Islington
will listen

Cleanse Kensington
& make healthy
Chelsea

Drinking condemns
Kingston upon Thames
gambling Lambeth
Opportunism Lewisham

Thirty-two

They're hurting
in Merton
inhuman in Newham

Redbridge is wreckage
Richmond ill-conditioned
Southwark is sick
Sutton is rotten

Scour the bandits of Tower Hamlets
and horrid Waltham Forest

Abscond, abandon
Wandsworth
infest Westminster

Thirty-two boroughs call to you

Parents Making Music

When he picks up his guitar
and she sits at the piano
and they play something together,
my parents are doing
almost exactly
what King David did, with the chief of the musicians.

God, please let them continue
to make music together
for many years.

Recording Device

Did King David, when Solomon
was little, make up songs
with him? And did he remember them?

Though a king, he lacked
devices available to an ordinary chap,
in the twenty-first century,

and can't have listened back
to the precise sound they made
singing together outdoors,

him and his little one.

Really Into It

I found a picture by Giotto
of the entry to Jerusalem.

Then I followed the precepts of St Ignatius
and put myself into the scene.

Not only using my imagination
but with actual paint.

Mind you, I'm no Giotto.
And I'm no saint.

Didn't take long to decide
that I don't belong among the disciples.

So I placed myself in the crowd
among the people bowing,

covering their heads. You'll find me
Towards the front, waving a palm, in specs.

Fresh Start Haiku

In the cemetery
Life whisks blossom from tree bones
To make its comeback.

Baiku

Pedalling, I sing:
'Glad that I live am I.' Yikes,
how embarrassing.

Regent's Park Flyover

Helicopters overhead
> watching criminals
>> or traffic

Also circling:
> the big festivals
>> of spring

On fragile rotors
> of daffodils
>> and forsythia

Passover, Chez Jesus

Imagine one happy moment
when Jesus, in his early years,
after dipping herbs in salty tears
won the hunt for the afikomen.
Picture him scoffing the egg,
watching Joseph
paint the tablecloth with ten signs,
a winedrop for each plague.
Share the gift of stories.
Lift the lamb bone.

99 Names

The sheikh stepped forward
shook hands, one hand on his heart.
They'd been drumming
when I knocked.

I imagined this large man
whirling around,
whirling in ecstasy.

He asked someone to bring me
orange juice.

Don't ask me to explain
why I came, who sent me.
Who sends anybody anywhere?

I was drawn here, magnetized
by what seemed like devotion.

I stayed till midnight,
chanting the 99 names of Allah
with men who called me brother.

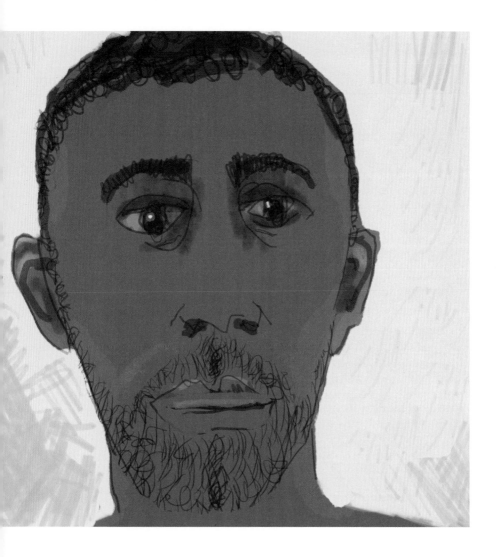

Soho Square

Lunchtime,
or just before.
A sunny day.
I stepped inside
the door
as I was on my way.

St Patrick's
Soho Square.
I didn't
exactly
go there
on a mission.

But passed
and asked
to see
Lucy
and pray
the rosary.

Where Do Ideas Come From?

If I have an idea
and it pleases me,
who deserves the credit?

Did I have the idea on purpose?

Or did it just arrive,
like sunshine falling on Primrose Hill?
Did God put it there?

If I think the thought,
another part of me
watches me
enjoying the thought.
Feeling clever.

Consciousness
becomes self-consciousness,
then self-absorption.

The watcher is cruel,
rarely gives credit,
always looks for flaws, loopholes, complacency;
as seems to have happened in this psalm.

Poetry

O God, you gave song
to the birds
and to us
you gave words
and how clever
to give words
a pattern of sounds
to help us remember.

Praise the Lord, for he gave us
rhyme, half-rhyme, feminine
rhyme, masculine rhyme, and
many other kinds, not to mention
alliteration and assonance.

And give thanks
for the schwa,
the inglorious sound
of a vowel
that has thrown in the towel.
The O in idiot,
the U in uh?
The glorious, inglorious
schwa.

Writing a poem or psalm
is exciting
not because of the thing
(the poem)
but because
without knowing
you find it
in writing.
It reveals itself as you go
like a statue to Michelangelo.

False Hope Haiku

'I will be happy
if they apologise first.'
Years passed. What a waste.

Unstressed

The unstressed syllable
walks behind the stressed.

The 'er' in partner,
the 'and' in husband,
the 'sort' in consort.

But on this day,
I watch the Queen

walk slowly behind
Prince Philip's coffin

and it hurts to watch.

List Making

All praise to God for lists,
for they help
impose order
on chaos.

When I'm feeling overwhelmed
I make lists.

Doesn't everybody?

Noah couldn't have marshalled
all those pairs of beasts and birds
without a list.

But no human brain could imagine the list
of every numbered hair,
and sparrow, and blade of grass,
etc.

What a list.

Genesis in Childs Hill

When we get online together
I show her the pictures I've made
of biblical scenes in the streets
nearby, using screengrabs
from Street View.

There's the picture
of Abraham entertaining angels
outside a terraced house on Crewys Road
(with Sarah peeking anxiously
through the net curtains
as they feast at a table by the bins).

The sketch of Moses
bringing down the tablets of the law
from Whitestone Pond,
the bush burning behind him
at approximately the place
where cars attempt to escape
from heavy traffic in rush hour.

And another drawing of Abraham,
preparing to sacrifice Isaac,
at the bottom of Ridge Road,
near the dry cleaner
on Cricklewood Lane.

She laughs, but not unkindly,
and I wonder
where else I can picture
the Bible in these streets.

Parables

I like the parables.
We're walking along together, talking,
and Splash! a story plops into the water
we didn't even know we swam in.
Not just any old story.
Hardly a story at all – a puzzle,
extended metaphor,
plug for a different socket,
coin for a different slot,
key to someone else's front door.
You take it, jiggle it about,
baffled, annoyed.
And then somehow you find a way
to make sparks fly, hit the jackpot, fling the door open.

Neighbours

Thank you for David at number 20,
  for his food bank collection

Thank you for Laura at number 30,
  for her work with children with autism

Thank you for Brian opposite,
  for his offer of a telly when we were burgled, for catching our
  rats and for clearing our drains

Thank you for Yvonne at number 7,
  for her enthusiasm, encouragement and coffee

Thank you, Martin next door,
  for inviting me to his club

Thank you, Barbara and Daniel,
  for warmth and cheerful good nature

Thank you, Preston and Suzanne at number 18,
  for our garden steps, and for support in neighbourhood
  projects

Thank you, Adam and Krysha at number 21,
  for always saying hi

Thank you, Lesley at 30, with your daughters,
  for your friendship and helpfulness

Thank you, Trevor and Denise, and Tina, and John and Jennifer, and Nigel, and Michael and Sylvia, and John and Adam, and Gillian, and newer neighbours I don't know yet, and others whose names I have temporarily forgotten, having already moved on (Nick!). Thank you for my neighbours, my people.

Dead Poets

Audenary

Sweep the filth of habit from my heart.
Scrub the grot of fortune off my past.

Ring the bells of Buddhists in my ears.
Beat the drums of Sufis through my fears.

Grant the prayers of Hindus
Bake the Jewish challah
Place the feet of Jains
Fill the rooms of Quakers
Bang the nails of Luther
Till we're one again

Rinse the soap of Scripture round my head.
Keep me in the care of all my dead.

George Herbert on Facebook

I dreamed I watched George Herbert preach today.
        He preached on Facebook Live,
He said that on a donkey Christ arrived
        To live for five more days.

George Herbert preached from West End Lane,
    A candle by his side
The congregation heard him say Christ died
    And add, 'We're all the same.'

God Bless Adrian Mitchell

God bless Adrian Mitchell
what he made up
and all that was factual

God bless Adrian Mitchell
the Arcadian songs
he pulled from his satchel

God bless Adrian Mitchell
from Tufnell Park
to a celestial recital

God bless Adrian Mitchell
the heart he expressed
with which you enrich all.

Reflection

The face of the waters
like a cheese grater
shreds the twilight, pink and mauve,
and distant headlights as they move.

The Integrated Self

How to describe the indescribable?
And why even bother?

All the descriptions in the world
Can't show the infinite.

Perhaps the best we can do is offer
A different way of thinking.

Baffle, instead of rationalize,
Like with one-hand clapping.

In daily life, you see a person laugh, cry, shout
But never all at once.

You never see the whole, integrated self.

God's a bit like that.

I only see God's footsteps,
Catch a heel as it disappears up the hall.

And contemplating this brings peace.
That's why I bother.

Pope Francis in Westminster

What is the quality of mercy?
Pope Francis
proposes some answers
in a Westminster Cathedral
bookshop book
I took up.

He says mercy makes real
chapter 16 of Ezekiel:
'The prophet speaks of shame
and shame is a grace.
Saint Ignatius
asked for shame
and God is gracious.'

We fear a loss, when we open our heart.

'I think of Father Carlos Duarte,
Ibarra, the confessor I saw in September
On St Matthew's feast day, 1953.
I felt God's mercy
and I remember
one year later, going home after
his funeral and burial.
I felt alone,
abandoned,
and I cried a lot
that night, really a lot. I hid.

I felt that I had lost a person who had
helped me feel the mercy of God.'

Only at the time do such encounters
seem like mere chances.
'Later we see that God's grace surrounds us.'

I bought the book by Pope Francis.

Weeds in June

Unwilling to hide any longer,
The weeds of north London make a daring escape,
Shooting up in glorious red, yellow and green
From the cracks in the pavement.

This has been their big year,
With garden centres all closed down.
On suburban estates amid the roses,
Weeds bend their elbows and crack knuckles.

Trellic Tower

At Panella on a pavement table
waiting for Mark,
the fastest man alive
when it comes to finding a reason
to thank God,
even and especially
when it all goes pear shaped.
I wonder if King David
wrote any psalms
while waiting for lunch
with a friend,
someone he loved,
and stared out across the pavements
at the people of Jerusalem
going about their business,
his pencil moving fast.

Retreat

After a difficult day
we went for a walk

as the blue turned black
over the city

and the red lights gleamed
on the tall buildings and cranes

and H. said
maybe you should go

on a retreat
to a monastery

and even the thought of it
was such a relief

Revelations

Waking with a jolt
of revelation
I realised that people who want evidence
☐ you exist
☐ where you hide
☐ your trick for sending sap up trees
☐ your knack for moulding clouds into interesting shapes
☐ the genetic code you write
☐ and the legal system behind your baffling offer of free will for all,
well, I realised
that those people
are welcome to pursue their inquiries.

I'm curious too.

But I value my faith.
I know it's only faith,
and I know it depends on
not knowing everything,
because otherwise it wouldn't be faith.

The L Is My S, I Shall Not W

The Lawn is my Square Mile, I shall not Wander

The Lifestyle is my Shackle, I shall not Whistle

The Ltd is my Shame, I shall not Whitewash

The Logo is my Sheol, I shall not Worship

The Litter is my Shadow, I shall not Waste

The Lyric is my Shiatsu, I shall not Wince

The Link is my Shortcut, I shall not Wait

The Loft is my St Paul's, I shall not Whine

The Laugh is my Shalom, I shall not Withhold

John-Paul's Letter to God

Dear Mr God, or Mrs/Ms

Thank you for your very generous gift, which I should have acknowledged many years ago.

I confess I didn't have the slightest idea how to use it, and actually somewhat regretted that you had even bothered to invent and force on me what appeared to be a machine for shutting down all kinds of fun every week, but experiment has helped me to use it as a thick duvet; noise-cancelling earphones; one of those inflatable neck supports used on long-haul flights; a cup of cocoa; a Persian rug; a big fat everlasting scented candle; and a fish tank (to stare at).

I confess that I have also broken off little bits of it, to nibble on throughout the week. When I do, I always think of you with gratitude.

I would be happy to share it, if you can think of anybody who might like some.

Yours faithfully

Write Your Own Psalm